P9-DFS-256

A Mom for Umande

by
Maria Faulconer

illustrated by
Susan Kathleen Hartung

Dial Books for Young Readers
an imprint of Penguin Group (USA) LLC

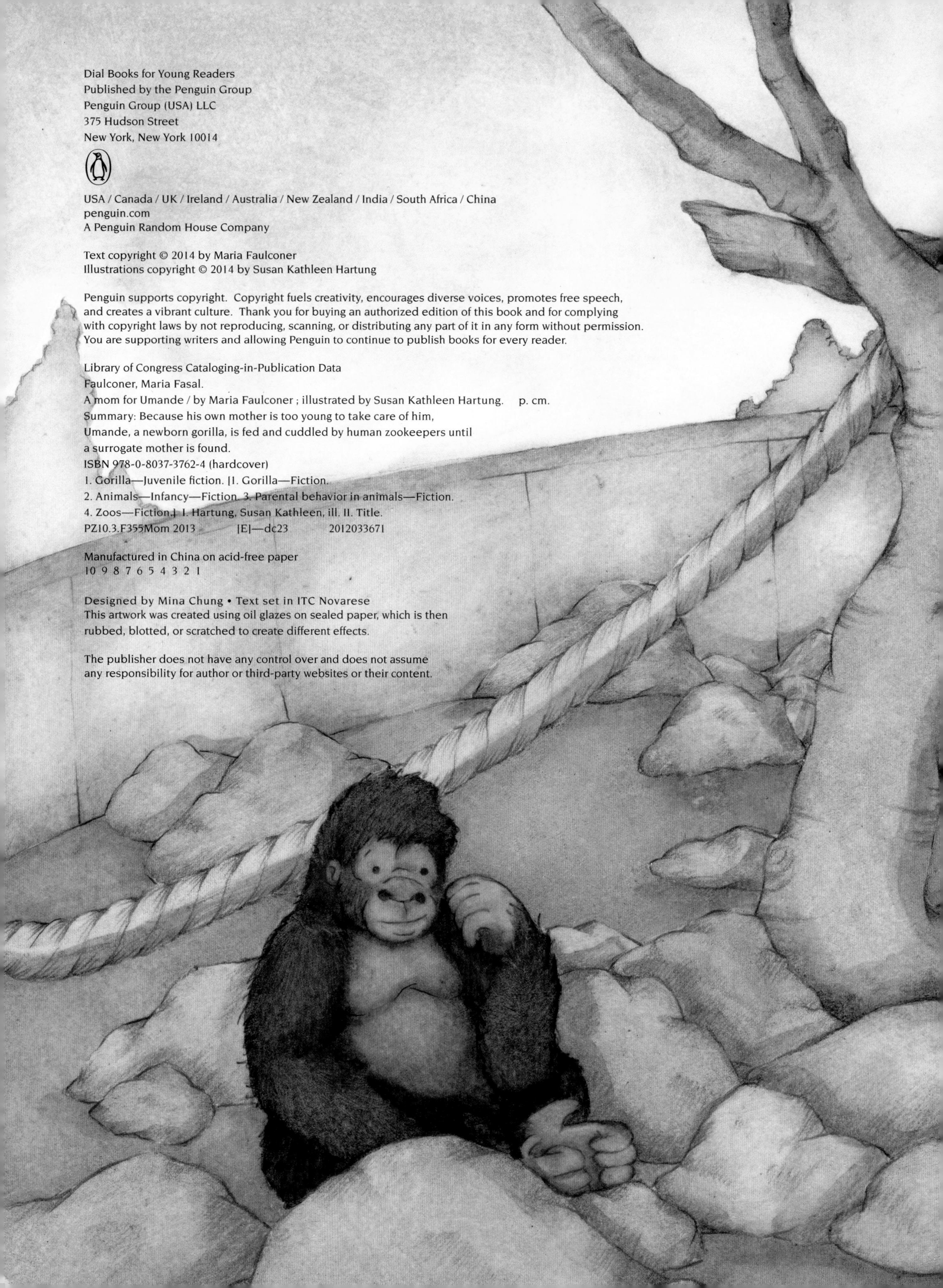

Dial Books for Young Readers
Published by the Penguin Group
Penguin Group (USA) LLC
375 Hudson Street
New York, New York 10014

USA / Canada / UK / Ireland / Australia / New Zealand / India / South Africa / China
penguin.com
A Penguin Random House Company

Library of Congress Cataloging-in-Publication Data
Faulconer, Maria Fasal.
A mom for Umande / by Maria Faulconer ; illustrated by Susan Kathleen Hartung. p. cm.
Summary: Because his own mother is too young to take care of him,
Umande, a newborn gorilla, is fed and cuddled by human zookeepers until
a surrogate mother is found.
ISBN 978-0-8037-3762-4 (hardcover)
1. Gorilla—Juvenile fiction. [1. Gorilla—Fiction.
2. Animals—Infancy—Fiction. 3. Parental behavior in animals—Fiction.
4. Zoos—Fiction.] I. Hartung, Susan Kathleen, ill. II. Title.
PZ10.3.F355Mom 2013 [E]—dc23 2012033671

Manufactured in China on acid-free paper
10 9 8 7 6 5 4 3 2 1

Designed by Mina Chung • Text set in ITC Novarese
This artwork was created using oil glazes on sealed paper, which is then rubbed, blotted, or scratched to create different effects.

For my children, Kristen
and Ryan, with love
–M.F.

For Mom & Dad
–S.K.H

On a cold winter's night, the zoo is quiet. The visitors have gone home. In the darkness of the Cheyenne Mountain Zoo, a baby gorilla is born. His name is Umande, which means "swirling mists" in Swahili.

Umande is wet and trembling.

He cries, as if to say "Will you hold me?"

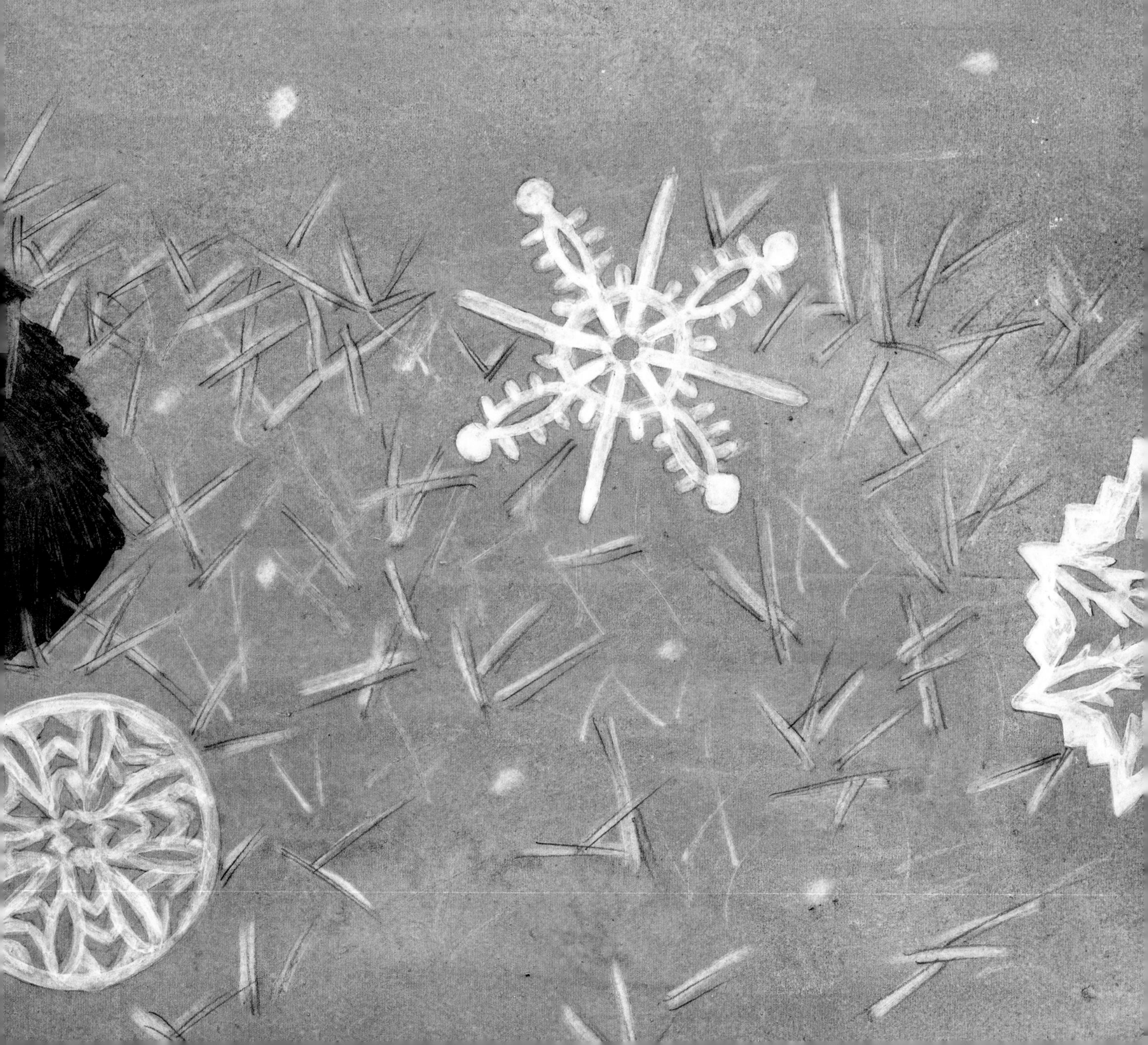

But Kwisha, his mother, doesn't. Several other gorillas come near him. But no one picks him up.

One of the keepers, Mandy, brings Umande to a nursery where she and the veterinarian take turns clutching him to their chests and wrapping blankets around him. They even give him sugar water from a bottle.

When he stops shivering, Mandy sets Umande back in the habitat.

He wiggles in a mound of sweet hay, smelling the musky odor of other gorillas, waiting for someone to pick him up.

But nobody does. Umande spends the night in the nursery.

During the day, two more keepers—Heidi and Debbie—take turns holding him up to a mesh wall, separating him from the gorilla area. The other gorillas sniff him and lick him. Especially Kwisha, his mother. She even comes when he cries. But when he's put in the area with her, she doesn't pick him up.

Kwisha is too young. She's never seen another baby gorilla, and she doesn't know what Umande needs.

So the keepers act as Umande's mom. Twenty-four hours a day, seven days a week, they teach him to be a gorilla.

Every day, Debbie takes him into a small habitat. She walks on her hands and knees, like his mother would, and carries him on her chest. He has to hold on tight to keep from falling.

She grooms him by removing imaginary dirt and bugs from his fur, his eyes, and even his nose.

When Umande cuts his first tooth, Heidi sits him on her lap and gives him bits of corn and apple. She drops crumbs on her lap, and he eats them.

She teaches him to make gorilla sounds. When she's happy with him she makes happy grumbles, which sound like *purrs*.

But when he's naughty and bites too hard, she coughs in his face. If he doesn't learn good gorilla manners, he could get hurt when he joins the other gorillas.

At night, Umande sleeps cuddled on Heidi's stomach or nestled against her side. She's warm and soft, but she's not his mother.

When the other gorillas are outside, Debbie takes Umande into the big gorilla habitat. She carries him on her back up ropes and onto log platforms. Sometimes, she hangs her hand down for him to grab.

Almost everything goes in his mouth.

Umande's favorite game is chase. He tags Debbie and runs away, as if to say "Are you coming?"

When she tickles him on his tummy, he throws his head back, closes his eyes, and falls backward in the hay.

Umande is happy at the zoo, but something is missing.

When Umande is almost seven months old, Heidi gives the gorillas who have shown the most interest in him one last chance to be his mom. When it's Kwisha's turn, Umande chases after her. Instead of picking him up, she swings him round and round.

Kwisha wants a playmate, but Umande needs a mom.

When Umande spends time with Rafiki, his dad, he's gentle and touches Umande nose to nose.

But, as head of his troop, Rafiki's job is to protect all the females. He's too concerned about them to take care of a baby gorilla.

So the keepers have to come up with a plan.

When Umande is eight months old, Heidi and Debbie bundle him up to take him away on an airplane. They pack formula, towels, sweet potatoes and greens, dog toys, and his favorite blankets. Umande sits on Heidi's lap and peeks out the window.

After flying all morning, they then travel in a van to the Columbus Zoo and Aquarium.

Heidi and Debbie take Umande into a special area with lots of hay, mesh walls, and climbing ropes. His new home smells just like his old one. But will he find a mom here?

A gorilla named Lulu is in a habitat two over from Umande's.

The minute they see each other they speak in a language all their own, full of quiet, happy grumbles.

Umande has to be separated from the other gorillas to allow Umande time to get aquainted with his new home, but every day, he goes to the mesh with Barb, his new keeper, and looks at Lulu.

Then after two weeks, he and Barb move into an area next to Lulu. Umande and Lulu touch fingers through the mesh. They even build nests across from each other.

But they can't be together yet.

Finally, after four weeks, Lulu and Umande are put in the same habitat.

They touch and smell each other. Lulu, being a very experienced mom, picks him up carefully.

They play peekaboo games
under the blankets.

They play with boxes.

When Barb walks by,
Lulu scoops Umande up
and shows him off.

When it's time to eat,
Umande perches on Lulu's head
to take his bottle.

After three days, they are never more than an inch apart.
Umande rides on Lulu's back.
When she lies down, she sets him on her belly.
They laugh their quiet gorilla laugh.

At night, when the zoo is quiet and the visitors have gone home, Lulu hangs her hand down and Umande grabs on. She takes him up to her nest. He curls beside her, and they fall asleep together.

At last, Umande has a mom.

A Mom for Umande is a love story between two gorillas—a baby named Umande, who was born at the Cheyenne Mountain Zoo in Colorado Springs, Colorado, and a forty-one-year-old named Lulu, who lived at the Columbus Zoo and Aquarium in Columbus, Ohio. How they found each other is a testament to the extraordinary dedication of a village of keepers, caregivers, and community volunteers at both zoos. I wish to thank them all—especially Sean Anglum, former Public Relations and Special Events Manager, and Dina Bredahl, Animal Care Manager, at the Cheyenne Mountain Zoo; as well as Dusty Lombardi, Senior Animal Care Adviser, and Barb Jones, keeper, at the Columbus Zoo and Aquarium—for the countless hours they spent teaching me about gorilla behavior. I could never have told this story without their enthusiastic and tireless support. Thanks, also, to the many photographers in Colorado Springs and Columbus whose thoughtfully captured images brought Umande and Lulu to life for me, especially Dave Liggett, Jerilee Bennett, Michael Pogany, and Tracey Gazibara. Finally, heartfelt thanks to my writer friends: first and foremost, Linda DuVal for sharing Umande with me, Emerita Anderson, Marty Banks, Nancy Bentley, Ann Black, Jimmie Butler, Mary Peace Finley, Toni Knapp, Barb Nickless, Denise Pomeraning, Carol Reinsma, and Susan Rust.

Author's Note

When I read a newspaper article about Umande and saw a photo of him snuggling with his adoptive mom, Lulu, I was captivated by the sheer joy on their faces. I'm an adoptive mom, too, and I knew right then that I had to write a story about this resilient little gorilla.

Since Umande had already been sent to the Columbus Zoo and Aquarium, I learned about him through interviews with keepers at both zoos. In the story, I singled out four keepers, but there were many more. During the eight months Umande lived at the Cheyenne Mountain Zoo, a total of eighteen keepers and caregivers spent thousands of hours taking care of him. When Umande came to the Columbus Zoo and Aquarium, experienced keepers continued teaching him to be a gorilla while caring for him around the clock.

The keeper staff at the Columbus Zoo and Aquarium is expert at infant gorilla care. Their hand-rearing plan for baby gorillas is world-renowned. In fact, the Cheyenne Mountain Zoo used their plan to teach Umande how to be a gorilla.

Sadly, Lulu died in 2011 at the age of forty-six. She will always be remembered for the joy she brought to Umande as his surrogate mom. Since 2012, Umande has been living in Chicago's Lincoln Park Zoo, where he is a member of their first bachelor group of western lowland gorillas.

If you're interested in learning more about gorillas, hand-rearing, or conservation programs, you may contact the Cheyenne Mountain Zoo at www.cmzoo.org, Chicago's Lincoln Park Zoo at www.lpzoo.org, or the Columbus Zoo and Aquarium at www.columbuszoo.org. To learn more about animal conservation in general, contact the World Wildlife Fund at www.worldwildlife.org.

DATE